FAMILY MATTERS –

(A Word to the Wise)

FAMILY MATTERS –
(A Word to the Wise)

David Pytches

eagle

Guildford, Surrey

British Library Cataloguing in Publication Data. A catalogue record for
this book is available from the British Library.

Published by Eagle Publishing Ltd, PO Box 530, Guildford, Surrey
GU2 4FH.

Typeset by Eagle Publishing
Printed by Cox & Wyman, Reading
ISBN No: 0 86347 512 4

CONTENTS

PREFACE

This book is part of a lifetime's collection and provides a resource for talks, addresses, after dinner speeches, sermons, and prose. Mainly it offers one liner jests and put-downs, worldly commonplaces and religious proverbs, besides some choice definitions and random flashes of insight. Just occasionally there has been a slight repitition of one or two of these one-liners where the quote has been applicable under either heading.

I have to offer my apologies to all those who are quoted in this book and have not been acknowledged. I often leave company savouring the humour, the cleverness, or the sound of some phrase and so rarely have remembered who said it first. I also want to thank all those whose original *bon mots* I have incorporated in this collection.

The proverb or wise saying is perhaps the most universal form of wisdom – (PROF DAVID F. FORD)

I look for something slightly quirky, maybe a quotation or something that shows a sense of humour – (DR BRENDA CROSS – ADMISSIONS TUTOR FOR THE MEDICAL SCHOOL, UNIVERSITY OF LONDON – AS REPORTED IN *THE DAILY TELEGRAPH* 4TH OCTOBER 2000)

There is no reason why a book of quotations should be dull; it has its uses in idleness as well as in study – (H.L. MENCKEN)

What a good thing Adam had. When he said a good thing he knew nobody had said it before – (MARK TWAIN)

I always have a quotation for everything – it saves original thinking – (DOROTHY L. SAYERS)

He liked those many literary cooks
Who skim the cream from others' books;
And ruin half their author's graces
By plucking bon mots from their places
– (HANNAH MORE)

Next to the originator of a good sentence is the first quoter from it – (RALPH WALDO EMERSON)

I know heaps of quotations, so I can always make quite a fair show of knowledge – (O. DOUGLAS)

AGE

To me old age is always fifteen years older than I am
– *(Bernard Baruch)*

The real trouble with old age is that it lasts for such
a short time – *(Sir John Mortimer)*

Middle age is when the broad mind and the narrow
waist change places – *(Anon)*

As a white candle in a holy place,
so is the beauty of an aged face
– *(Anon)*

I am a young man renting an old man's body –
(Senior citizen)

If I had known I was going to live so long I would
have taken better care of myself – *(Leon Eldred)*

They spend their time mostly looking forward to the past – *(John Osborne)*

She may very well pass for forty-three,
in the dusk with the light behind her
– *(W.S. Gilbert)*

Seen it all, done it all; can't remember most of it – *(Anon)*

All I have to live on now is macaroni and memorial services – *(Margaret Asquith)*

I've lived a wonderful life, met wonderful people, been to wonderful places – but I'm getting old. It seems it (life) ought to be before me but it's all gone – gone like a flash! – *(Stewart Granger interviewed by Michael Parkinson)*

Here's to you. No matter how old you are, you don't look it – *(Anon)*

I want to grow up before I grow old – *(John Wimber)*

My goal is to become a very old man as slowly as possible – *(Senior citizen)*

When a man falls into his anecdotage its time for him to retire – *(Benjamin Disraeli)*

Nostalgia is all right, but it's not what it used to be – *(Graffito)*

You know you are getting old when you stoop to tie your shoes and wonder what else you can do while you're down there – *(George Burns)*

Three 'R's of old age – Rambling, Reminiscence and Repetition – *(John Eddison)*

Man has four ages
  – lager
     – aga
         – Saga
             and ga-ga – *(Anon)*

We do not count men's years until he has nothing else to count – *(Ralph Waldo Emerson)*

A person is always startled when he seriously hears himself called an old man for the first time – *(Oliver W. Holmes)*

Your old age begins and middle life ends, the day your descendants outnumber your friends – *(Ogden Nash)*

To be seventy years young is sometimes more cheerful and hopeful than to be forty years old – *(Oliver W. Holmes)*

Every man desires to live long; but no man would be old – *(Dean Swift)*

It's frustrating to know all the answers, but nobody is asking the questions – *(Anon)*

My glass shall not persuade me I am old – *(William Shakespeare)*

Nothing is more beautiful than cheerfulness in old age – *(Richter)*

Beautiful young people are accidents of nature. Beautiful old people are works of art – *(Eleanor Roosevelt)*

The seven ages of man:

> spills,
> drills,
> thrills,
> bills,
> ills,
> pills,
> wills. – *(Richard J. Needham)*

The first forty years of life give us the text: the next seventy supply the commentary – *(A. Schopenhauer)*

What makes old age hard to bear . . . is the burden of one's memories – *(Somerset Maugham)*

I'm very proud of my gold pocket watch. My grandfather, on his death bed, sold me this watch – *(Woody Allen)*

Ageing – and even death may no longer be inevitable – *(Prof John Harris Report on Bio-ethics 7th April 2000)*

At my age flowers scare me – *(George Burns)*

A 102-year-old woman was asked whether she had any worries. 'No, I haven't,' she replied. 'Not since my youngest son went into an old folks home.' – *(Anon)*

There are three stages of man: he believes in Santa Claus, he does not believe in Santa Claus, he is Santa Claus. – *(Bob Phillips)*

The most delightful advantage of being bald: one can hear snowflakes – *(R.G. Daniels)*

Joan Collins has discovered the secret of eternal middle age – *(Anon)*

Middle age is when you get enough exercise just avoiding people who think you should be getting more – *(Anon)*

Middle age is when you choose your cereal for the fibre, not for the toy – *(Anon)*

Man has four ages
　– Infancy
　　– Childhood
　　　– Adolescence
　　　　– Obsolescence – *(Art Linkletter)*

Nancy Reagan has had a face lift. Joan Collins uses a fork lift – *(Anon)*

'We have something which can correct your hearing, Madam.' 'Forget it – I'm eighty-nine and I have already heard enough!' – *(Old lady to salesman)*

He thinks himself deaf because he no longer hears himself talked of. – *(Charles Maurice de Talleyrand-Périgord)*

It was said of Principal Rainy that 'he had the secret of perennial youth' – *(Anon)*

Age is a high price to pay for maturity – *(Anon)*

He had one foot in the grave and the other on a banana skin – *(Anon)*

My mind not only wanders – sometimes it leaves me completely – *(Anon)*

You know you are over the hill when it takes longer to rest than it took to get tired – *(Anon)*

I am lonesome. They are all dying. I have hardly a warm personal enemy left – *(James McNeill Whistler)*

Growing old is mandatory; growing up is optional – *(Anon)*

A man once complained that it was awful growing old alone – his wife had not had a birthday in fourteen years! – *(Anon)*

You're getting old when you get the same sensation from a rocking chair that you once got from a roller coaster – *(Anon)*

ANCESTORS

Whoever serves his country well has no need of ancestors – *(Voltaire)*

It's not what you get from your ancestors but what you leave for your descendants that matters – *(Anon)*

Every time I look up my family tree they throw nuts down
– *(Anon)*

I come from a very old military family. One of my ancestors fell at Waterloo. Someone pushed him off Platform Nine – *(Eric Morecambe)*

I have royal blood in my veins – yes, my grandmother was stung by a queen bee! – *(Anon)*

BABIES

Babies – angels whose wings grow shorter as their legs grow longer – *(Anon)*

Ours was a perfect baby – he had obviously read all the books – *(Anon)*

Everyone knows how to raise children except the parents who have them – *(P.J. O'Rourke)*

BATHROOM, TOILET

There is only one immutable law in life – in a gentleman's toilet, incoming traffic has the right of way – *(Hugh Leonard)*

First left, go along the corridor. You'll see a door marked Gentlemen, but don't let that deter you – *(F.E. Smith)*

At this moment you are the only man in the Church of England who knows what he is doing. – *(Graffito in the Gents!)*

BUILDING

Don't clap too hard – it's a very old building – (Graffito)

The lift is being fixed for the day. During that time we regret that you will be unbearable – *(Notice in Bucharest hotel lobby)*

So I rang up my local building firm and said 'I want a skip outside my house,' and he said, 'I'm not stopping you!' – *(Anon)*

CHILDREN

Suffer the little children to come unto me, and forbid them not: for of such is the kingdom of God – *(Mark 10:14 – KJV)*

Our children are like library books on loan with a due date that remains unknown – *(Jane Brooks)*

Insanity is hereditary; you can get it from your children – *(Sam Levenson)*

Children are natural mimics who act like their parents despite every effort to teach them good manners – *(Anon)*

Anyone who has survived his childhood has enough information about life to last him the rest of his days – *(Flannery O'Connor)*

The great man is he who does not lose his child-heart – *(Mencius)*

Having one child makes you a parent; having two makes you a referee – *(David Frost)*

The worst things that can ever happen to a child:
1. Always to have its own way.
2. Never to have its own way – *(Anon)*

Bedtime is the oldest argument in the world – *(Juliet Janvrin)*

Sweet childish days, that were as long
As twenty days are now
– *(William Wordsworth –*
To a Butterfly*)*

I hope it doesn't rain today. I just hate it when the children play inside – *(Two female kangaroos in conversation)*

I'll thcream, and I'll thcream and I'll thcream till I'm thick – *(Richmal Crompton – Violet Elizabeth Bott's continual threat in her William books)*

A parent is a sandbank that holds back the tide of life until the child is ready to swim – *(Juliet Janvrin)*

The greatest security for children is to have parents who invest in their own relationship – *(Juliet Janvrin)*

The proper time to influence the character of a child is about a hundred years before he is born – *(Ralph William Inge* – The Observer*)*

There's only one pretty child in the world and every mother has it – *(Proverb)*

There are no illegitimate children – only illegitimate parents – *(Leon R. Yankwich)*

Research shows that children play better in a playground with a fence – *(Anon)*

We spend more than £250 on average for every child in the land on Christmas presents alone – *(John Humphreys* – Devil's Advocate*)*

The cost of bringing up a child for a family was £3,000 a year each – *(Loughborough University study 1977)*

Parenting is one of the most expensive pursuits open to humanity – *(Juliet Janvrin)*

The quickest way for a parent to get a child's attention is to sit down and look comfortable – *(Lane Olinghouse* – in the* Wall Street Journal*)*

While providing our kids with what we didn't have we can deprive them of what we did have – *(Anon)*

The burden of being unforgiven is too heavy for young shoulders – *(Juliet Janvrin)*

Families are like fudge . . . mostly sweet, with a few nuts – *(Anon)*

We spend the first twelve months of our children's lives teaching them to walk and talk and the next twelve telling them to sit down and shut up – *(Phyllis Diller)*

A child without discipline will
fight our failure to set boundaries
by behaving badly
– *(Juliet Janvrin)*

There is no end to the violations committed by children on children, quietly talking alone – *(Elizabeth Bowen* – The House of Paris*)*

Train up a child in the way he should go: and when he is old, he will not depart from it – *(Proverbs 22:6 – KJV)*

Calm words . . . calm children – *(Juliet Janvrin)*

The average child probably sees 10,000 commercials a year – *(John Humphreys* – Devil's Advocate*)*

Empty promises undermine
a child's trust
– (Juliet Janvrin)

I want my children to have all the little things I could never afford and then I want to move in with them – *(Anon)*

Never underestimate your importance as a parent – *(Juliet Janvrin)*

Sometimes we are so concerned about giving our children what we never had growing up, we neglect to give them what we did have growing up – *(James Dobson)*

Watching your daughter being collected by her date feels like handing over a million dollar Stradivarius to a gorilla – *(Jim Bishop)*

I want my children to know that I fought for something worthwhile! – *(Anon)*

Having children is not a leap into the dark – it's a leap into the future – *(Juliet Janvrin)*

The most important thing a father can do for his children is to love their mother – *(Anon)*

You're better than just a father. You're a DADDY – *(Little girl looking her father in the face)*

I did not know what God looked like so I just drew a picture of my daddy – *(Little girl)*

If a child is attention seeking give him some attention – *(Juliet Janvrin)*

Being a father is part joy and part guerilla warfare – *(quoted on TV by Steve Chalke)*

Getting into bed makes a child thirsty – *(Juliet Janvrin)*

What's done to children, they will do to society – *(Dr Karl Menninger)*

I try to remember that my father was somebody's child – *(Anon)*

The calf cannot imagine what it's like being a cow and the cow can't remember what it was like being a calf – *(Martin Luther)*

There are only two lasting bequests we can give our children. One is roots and the other is wings – *(Hodding Carter)*

Training a child to follow the straight and narrow way is easy for parents. All they have to do is lead the way – *(Anon)*

The prevalence of juvenile delinquency is proving that parents are not getting at the seat of the problem – *(Anon)*

Never leave a child crying in the night – *(Juliet Janvrin)*

After dinner a lot of family members suffer from dish-temper – *(Anon)*

Only a grandparent can be as fascinated by a child's development as its parents – *(Juliet Janvrin)*

It is a wise parent who can occasionally admit his or her own failings to a child – *(Juliet Janvrin)*

Unless we reach our children's hearts today, they will break our hearts tomorrow – *(Anon)*

A two-year-old's temper tantrum is the first great rebellion of life – *(Anon)*

A child is likely to see God as Father if he sees God in his father – *(Anon)*

Having a family is like having a bowling alley installed in your head – *(Martin Mull)*

Children need our encouragement above all other rewards – *(Anon)*

Children often demand 'Yes' when they long for 'No' – *(Juliet Janvrin)*

My mother told my father that we were ruining the front lawn playing on it. My father replied, 'We're raising kids, not grass!' – *(Harmon Killebrew when elected to the Baseball Hall of Fame in 1984)*

September is when millions of bright shining happy laughing faces turn toward school. They belong to mothers! – *(Anon)*

An angry child has no inhibitions – *(Juliet Janvrin)*

When I went up to the communion rails with my daddy, the man said 'Bless you' and I hadn't even sneezed – *(Little girl)*

There is just one way to bring up a child in the way he should go, and that is to travel that way yourself – *(Abraham Lincoln)*

It is easy to humiliate children, but hard to build their self-esteem – *(Juliet Janvrin)*

Sons are a heritage from the LORD – *(Psalm 127:3 – NIV)*

When children lose self-control, they need your control to find it again – *(Juliet Janvrin)*

Who holds the souls of children, holds the nation – *(Anon)*

Children are a life's work – *(Juliet Janvrin)*

Reward a child's achievement – *(Juliet Janvrin)*

Children are so inoculated with small doses of Christianity that they seldom catch the real thing – *(George Bernard Shaw)*

Children's dreams encapsulate their fears and hopes. Take time to listen to them – *(Juliet Janvrin)*

Before I was married I had three theories about raising children. Now I have three children and no theories – *(John Wilmot – the Earl of Rochester)*

For children uniformity is social acceptance – *(Juliet Janvrin)*

My Grandma is like the sun when it's dull. She comes out and brightens up the day – *(Greg Munro aged 8½)*

Children need imaginary superheroes – *(Juliet Janvrin)*

My grandma is like a special treasure to me and I keep her safe in my heart – *(Victoria Graham aged 8)*

Our children are like mirrors – they reflect our attitudes in life – *(Anon)*

CLASS

Upper Crust! – a lot of crumbs held together by dough – *(Anon)*

Class distinction is only temporary. All men are cremated equal – *(Graffito)*

The test of a man or woman of breeding is how they behave in a quarrel – *(George Bernard Shaw)*

He is very cultured ... he can bore you on any subject – *(Anon)*

A gentleman never eats – he breakfasts,
he lunches,
he dines
but he never eats – *(Anon)*

Beware of the pursuit of the superman: it leads to an indiscriminate contempt for the human – *(George Bernard Shaw)*

Whether blue blood was in his veins is of small consequence, since we know that he was the seed royal of the redeemed of the Lord – *(Charles Spurgeon on Thomas Watson)*

If you bed with people of below-stairs class, they will go to the papers – *(Jane Clark)*

ETIQUETTE, MANNERS & PROTOCOL

Etiquette is knowing how to yawn with your mouth closed – *(Anon)*

Manners Maketh Man – *(Winchester School Motto)*

A gentleman knows how to play the accordion, but doesn't – *(Anon)*

Good manners are made up of petty sacrifices – *(Ralph Waldo Emerson)*

The test of good manners is to be patient with bad ones – *(Solomon Ibr Gabiroi)*

FAMILY

As the family goes, so goes the nation and so goes the world in which we live – *(Pope John Paul II – The Observer 1986)*

Treasure your families – the future of humanity passes by way of the family – *(Pope John Paul II – Speech 1982)*

The family that prays together stays together – *(Al Scalpone in the RC Family Rosary Crusade 1947)*

A family altar can alter a family – *(Anon)*

The family that feels together heals together – *(Anon)*

There are only two lasting bequests we can give our children. One is roots and the other is wings – *(Hodding Carter)*

For every child with a spark of genius there are a dozen with ignition trouble – *(Anon)*

Accidents will occur in the best of families – *(Charles Dickens in* David Copperfield*)*

Our families often know us best, but rarely do they know the best of us – *(Kate Chisolm)*

Other things may change us but we start and end with the family – *(Anthony Brandt)*

They were a tense and peculiar family, the Oedipuses, weren't they? – *(Sir Max Beerbohm)*

All that a child can expect is that its father be present at the conception – *(Joe Orton)*

No nation has ever prospered in which the family was not held sacred – *(Dean Inge)*

Take a child before he is seven and teach him well the way to heaven – *(Church maxim)*

By the age of three parents have done half of what they will ever do for their children – *(C.H. Benson)*

Parenting is not a job from which you can become redundant – *(Juliet Janvrin)*

FRIENDS

The only sure way to destroy your enemies is to make them your friends – *(Anon)*

[Friends are God's] apology for relations – *(Hugh Kingsmill)*

Do not use a hatchet to remove a fly from your friend's forehead
– *(Chinese Proverb)*

True friends trust each other – *(A.W. Tozer)*

Many people walk in and out of your life – but only true friends leave footprints in your heart – *(Eleanor Roosevelt)*

I detest him now more than cold *veal* – *(Lord Macaulay)*

He could fit all his friends into my
downstairs loo!
Is that with the lid up
or down?
– *(Paul Bougourd)*

To have a friend one must be a friend – *(Anon)*

To have a friend one must close one eye. To keep him – two – *(Norman Douglas)*

To make friends one must show oneself friendly – *(Solomon)*

You can't *find* the right person. You have to *become* the right person – *(Anon)*

You can make more friends in two months by becoming interested in other people than you can in two years by trying to get other people interested in you – *(Dale Carnegie)*

Always label the Christmas presents you receive. Then you won't give them back to the same friends next Christmas

– (Anon)

There are no true friends in politics. We are all sharks circling, and waiting for traces of blood to appear – *(Alan Clarke MP on political intrigue)*

Greater love hath no man than this, that he lay down his friends for his life – *(Jeremy Thorpe – one time leader of the Liberal Party)*

To our best friends, who know the worst about us but refuse to believe it. – *(Anon)*

I like to visit my friends from time to time just to look over my library – *(William Hazlitt)*

He was a great patriot, a humanitarian, a loyal friend – provided of course he really is dead – *(Voltaire)*

Friends are generally of the same sex for when men and women agree it is only for their conclusions; their reasons are always different – *(George Santayana)*

One out of four people is mentally unbalanced. Think of your three closest friends. If they seem OK then you're the one – *(Ann Landers)*

A good friend is a reflection of yourself, a mirror in which you see yourself – *(John Aspinall)*

There are two sorts of people in the world: the people anyone can live with and the people no one can live with – *(George Bernard Shaw)*

Grief can take care of itself but to get the full value of a joy it must be shared – *(Mark Twain)*

A friend is one who walks in when the rest of the world walks out – *(Walter Winchel)*

The worst solitude is to be destitute of sincere friendship – *(Francis Bacon)*

I no doubt deserved my enemies. I don't believe I deserve my friends – *(Walt Whitman)*

Life is nothing without friendship – *(Cicero)*

'Friend' derives from a word meaning 'free'. A friend is someone who allows us the space and freedom to be – *(Debbie Alicen)*

A friend never says 'I told you so' even when she did – *(Anon)*

True friendship comes when silence between two is comfortable – *(Dave Tyson Gentry)*

A friend is a person with whom you dare to be yourself – *(Pam Brown)*

A friend is someone who dislikes the same people you dislike – *(Anon)*

There's a miracle called friendship
That dwells within the heart
And you don't know
how it happens
Or how it gets its start
But the happiness it brings you
Always gives a special lift
And you realise that friendship
Is God's most precious gift
– *(Anon)*

GARDEN, GARDENING & FLOWERS

My neighbour asked if he could use my lawnmower? I told him that of course he could – so long as he didn't take it out of my garden! – *(Eric Morecambe)*

To get the best results you must talk to your vegetables – *(Prince Charles in TV interview 1986)*

Won't you come into the garden? I would like my roses to see you – *(Attributed to Richard Brinsley Sheridan)*

With nineteen gardeners, Lord Talbot of Malahide has produced an affair exactly like a suburban golf course – *(Nancy Mitford)*

I don't mind gardening but I just don't want to be there when it happens – *(Anon – with apologies to Woody Allen)*

Laid to lawn! This is laid to adventure playground! – *(Basil Boothroyd)*

I once had a rose named after me and I was very flattered. But I was not pleased to read the description in the catalogue; no good in bed, but fine up against a wall – *(Eleanor Roosevelt)*

For any garden, however small, one should set aside two or three acres of woodland – *(Anon lecturer on gardens)*

All really grim gardeners possess a keen sense of humus – *(W.C. Sellar)*

Perennials are the ones that grow like weeds, biennials are the ones that die this year instead of next, and hardy annuals are the ones that never come up at all – *(Katharine Whitehorn)*

HOLIDAYS

I suppose we all have our recollections
of our earlier holidays, all
bristling with horror
– *(Flan O'Brien)*

HOME

The strength of the nation derives from the integrity of the home – *(Confucius)*

An Englishman's home is his castle – *(Proverb)*

The most influential of all educational factors is the conversation in a child's home – *(William Temple)*

Mr Talkative was a saint abroad but a devil at home
– *(John Bunyan)*

Be not honey abroad and wormwood at home –
(Anon)

She's leaving home,
after living alone
for so many years
– *(song by John Lennon and Paul McCartney)*

The crown of the home is godliness – *(Anon)*

A man may buy a house but only a woman can make
it a home – *(Anon)*

My idea of housework is to sweep the room with a
glance – *(Anon)*

A man . . . is so in the way in the house! – *(Elizabeth
Gaskell)*

I hate housework! You make the beds, you do the dishes – and six months later you have to start all over again – *(Joan Rivers)*

Home is like an extended over coat – *(BBC Radio 4 comment)*

Home is the girl's prison and the woman's workhouse – *(George Bernard Shaw)*

If your Christianity does not work at home don't export it – *(Howard Hendricks)*

What makes a fire so pleasant is that it is a live thing in a dead room – *(Sydney Smith)*

Home wasn't built in a day – *(Anon)*

Home is where the heart is – *(Anon)*

A man's home may seem to be his castle on the outside; inside, it is more often his nursery – *(Clare Boothe Luce)*

The great advantage of a hotel is that it's a refuge from home life – *(George Bernard Shaw)*

Be nice to your kids. They'll choose your nursing home – *(Anon)*

The light that shines the furthest shines the brightest nearest home – *(Anon)*

There will be a special prize for the one who goes home first – *(Distraught hostess at children's birthday party)*

What's the good of a home if you are never in it? – *(George Grossmith)*

In the world the Christians are a colony of the true home – *(Dietrich Bonhoeffer)*

Home is the one place which when you go there they have to take you in – *(Robert Frost)*

It takes a heap o'livin in a house to make it home – *(Rudyard Kipling)*

The house was so dirty that you had to wipe your feet before you came out – *(Anon)*

A woman's place is in the wrong – *(Gordon Shaw)*

A woman's place in the House and the Senate – *(Anon)*

Conran's Law of Housework – it expands to fill the time available plus half an hour – *(Shirley Conran –* Superwoman*)*

Everything's getting on top of me. I can't switch off.
I've got a self-cleaning oven – I have to get up in the
night to see if it's doing it – *(Victoria Wood)*

Hatred of domestic work is a natural and admirable result of civilisation
– (Rebecca West)

Chinese script character for peace is one woman under one roof.
Chinese script character for war is three women under one roof – *(Anon)*

HOSPITALITY & INVITATIONS

Guests, like fish, stink after three days – *(Anon)*

The most welcome guest is the one who knows
when it's time to go home – *(Anon)*

Some people can stay longer in an hour than others can in a week – *(William D. Howells)*

Frank Harris has been invited to every great house in England – once. – *(Oscar Wilde)*

I regret very much my inability to attend your banquet. It is the baby's night out and I must stay at home with the nurse – *(Ring Lardner)*

LUXURY

Every luxury was lavished on you: atheism, breastfeeding, circumcision – *(Joe Orton)*

MAN

To know man we must begin with God – *(A.W. Tozer)*

Is man an ape or an angel? I'm on the side of the angels – *(Benjamin Disraeli)*

He looked like a man being led to the shopping block – *(Anon)*

A genius is a man who can rewrap a new shirt and not have any pins left over – *(Dino Levi)*

The ideal man does not exist: it's easier to find a husband – *(Brigette Eckhardt)*

God often does very good work with very poor tools – *(Bishop J.C. Ryle)*

Every man is a book if you know how to read him – *(Anon)*

The way to a man's pocketbook is through his hobby – *(Anon)*

Men are those creatures with two legs and eight hands – *(Jane Mansfield)*

I have never got over the fact that I was born in bed with a woman – *(Wilson Mizner)*

Man is the measure of all things – *(Protagoras)*

Men seldom make passes
at girls who wear glasses
– *(Dorothy Parker – 1937)*

Jesus Christ is a Man who came to save men – *(A.W. Tozer)*

God and men exist for each other and neither is satisfied without each other – *(A.W. Tozer)*

Men are looking for better methods – God is looking for better men – *(Anon)*

. . . the world moves on and times change but people remain the same always – *(A.W. Tozer)*

When he dances he's all feet and when he stops he's all hands – *(Female about Arthur Skeekman)*

MARRIAGE

The Bible teaches that marriage is God's idea rather than ours . . . – *(John Stott)*

(Marriage) is a heterosexual, monogamous and ideally lifelong partnership, expressing love and companionship; and that is the God-given context for sexual enjoyment and procreation and nurture of children . . . – *(John Stott)*

Most marriages die with a whimper as people run away from one another, slowly growing apart – *(John Gottman)*

Some say it's love that makes the marriage go round but in fact it's marriage that makes the love go round – *(Old adage)*

Love and marriage
Love and marriage
Go together like a horse and carriage
— *(Sammy Cahn)*

Too many people prepare for their weddings but not for their marriages — *(Anon)*
Marry in haste: repent at leisure — *(Proverb)*

All tragedies are finished by a death; all comedies are finished by a marriage — *(Proverb)*

If one is not caressed one develops thorns — *(Mrs Thrale)*

Marriage is better for raising children because unmarried couples are more abusive, unfaithful and unhealthy than married ones — *(Summary of findings from a huge seven-year survey of the Institute for Social and Economic Research)*

You don't love a woman because she is beautiful. She is beautiful because you love her – *(John and Anne Coles)*

Adam was created first . . . to give him a chance to say something – *(Anon)*

You are right dear! I'm so sorry! – *(Husband's appropriate response to wife for all occasions)*

I could never understand why my wife wanted a divorce – I always put her under a pedestal – *(Woody Allen)*

Marriage is a creative conflict – *(Anon)*

We got better at avoiding the minefields – now just to be in the same room gives us pleasure – *(Dame Judi Dench about her marriage to Michael Williams)*

If Adam and Eve were alive today they would probably sue the snake – *(Bern Williams)*

Lord Bolton has married Mrs Lavinia Fenton in Scotland, during a break in the fishing – *(The Times announcing Lord Bolton's third marriage)*

I'm sure he will be able to find a new wife to be unfaithful to soon – *(Anon of a serial adulterer)*

Adam blamed Eve and Eve blamed the serpent and the serpent didn't have a leg to stand on – *(Just one of those sayings)*

The Lord made Adam
The Lord made Eve
He made 'em both
a little naive
– *(E.Y. Young)*

He was engaged to a contortionist but she broke it off – *(Anon)*

The trouble for most married women is sex – too much of it or too little – *(Anon)*

Our courtship was fast and furious – I was fast and she was furious – *(Max Fanffman)*

Ah Mozart! He was happily married but his wife wasn't – *(Victor Borge)*

Ever since I said 'I do' there are a lot of things you don't – *(Anon)*

You can't *find* the right person. You have to *become* the right person – *(Anon)*

The world has grown suspicious of anything that looks like a happily married life – *(Oscar Wilde)*

Recently married. Wife knows everything – *(Newspaper advertisement)*

Marriage isn't a word . . . it's a sentence – *(King Vidor)*

He is dreadfully married. He's the most married man I ever saw in my life – *(Artemus Ward of the Mormon leader Brigham Young)*

Who gave the bride away? Well any of us could have done but we all decided to keep our mouths shut!

– (Guest's comment)

She cried – and the judge wiped her tears with my cheque book – *(Tommy Manville, thirteen times divorced American millionaire)*

It is a woman's business to get married as soon as possible, and man's to keep unmarried as long as he can – *(George Bernard Shaw)*

Holy deadlock
– (A.P. Herbert)

A good marriage consists in two good forgivers –
(Gigi Graham Tchividjian)

Often the difference between a successful marriage
and a mediocre one is leaving three or four things
unsaid – *(John and Anne Coles)*

A man may be a fool and not know it – but not if he
is married – *(H.L. Mencken)*

John Donne
Anne Donne
Un-done
*– (John Donne in a letter to his wife on being
dismissed from the service of his father-in-law)*

If we allow ourselves to become preoccupied with
divorce and its grounds, rather than with marriage
and its ideals, we lapse into Pharisaism – *(John Stott)*

The critical period in matrimony is breakfast time –
(A.P. Herbert)

Winter in England is so cold I almost got married –
(Attributed to Jenny Winters)

If you are afraid of loneliness, don't marry –
(Chekhov)

A couple in Hollywood got divorced. Then they got
remarried. The divorce didn't work out! – *(Anon)*

The formula for a successful marriage is
the same as in car manufacturing. I stick
to one model – *(Henry Ford)*

Marriage is like a bank account – you put in, you
take out and you lose interest – *(Anon)*

Marriage is the only war where one sleeps with the
enemy – *(Anon)*

We remain very married – *(Richard Gere and Cindy
Crawford following rumours of their separation)*

A man in love is incomplete until he's married –
then he's finished – *(Zsa Zsa Gabor)*

Marriage is a great institution but I am not ready for
an institution yet – *(Mae West)*

He taught me house-keeping; when I divorce him I
keep the house – *(Zsa Zsa Gabor)*

You become a semi non-person when you get married – *(Legendary feminist Ms Gloria Steinem who has recently married)*

Bigamy is having one husband too many. Monogamy is the same – *(Anon)*

Marriage is popular because it provides the maximum of temptation with the maximum of opportunity – *(George Bernard Shaw)*

Behind every successful man is a woman – and behind her is his wife – *(Groucho Marx)*

Marriage is a man-trap baited with simulated accomplishments and delusive idealizations – *(George Bernard Shaw)*

When women marry, they think their husbands will change. When men marry they think their wives will never change – *(Anon)*

No husband has ever been shot while doing the dishes – *(Anon)*

Marriages are made in heaven – *(Alfred Lord Tennyson)*

Every meaningful relationship requires significant communication – *(Anon)*

A woman's best protection is the right man – *(Clare Boothe Luce)*

Marriage starts when she sinks in his arms and ends with her arms in the sink – *(Anon)*

Fire needs a fireplace: sex needs marriage – *(Andy Comiskey)*

You have to kiss a lot of frogs before you find your prince – *(Despairing young lady)*

Girl: If we become engaged will you give me a ring?
Boy: Certainly! What is your number? – *(Anon)*

To Margaret, my wife, with whom it is as easy to stay in love as it was to fall in love – *(W.E. Sangster – Book dedication)*

There were three of us in this marriage so it was a bit crowded – *(Diana, Princess of Wales – BBC Panorama interview, 20th November 1995)*

I haven't reported my missing credit card to the police because whoever stole it is spending less than my wife – *(Illie Nastase)*

I did not marry my wife because she had four million. I would have married her if she only had two million – *(Charles Forte)*

He kissed me as though he was trying to clear the drains – *(Alida Baxter)*

My love life is so bad I'm taking part in the world celibacy championships. I meet the Pope in the semi-finals – *(Guy Bellamy)*

Basically my wife was immature. I'd be home in my bath and she'd come in and sink my boats – *(Woody Allen)*

I always wanted to marry Miss Wright but I never guessed she would be Always Right! – *(Anon)*

I learned how my wife ticks when she began to tock! – *(Ogden Nash)*

I have been faithful to you, Cynara, after my fashion – *(Ernest Dowson)*

A wedding does not equip one for marriage – *(Anon)*

A guest was late for Oscar Wilde's wedding and sent a telegram to the church: 'I am detained – don't wait!' – *(James McNeill Whistler)*

Never marry for money, darling, but marry where money is! – *(A mother)*

Marriage is when you get to keep your girl and don't have to give her back to the parents – *(Eric – aged 6)*

Tell your wife she looks pretty even if she looks like a truck – *(Ricky aged 10 – advice on making a marriage work)*

Eileen, dearest friend and devoted wife – *(Archbishop George Carey –* Canterbury Letters*)*

MATURITY

Maturity is a high price to pay for growing up – *(Tom Stoppard)*

MEDICINE, HEALTH & DOCTORS

I just can't bear to run short of Acetylmethyl-dimethyloxamidphenylhydrazine – *(James Agate – having gone on a trip and forgotten his 'asthma stuff')*

Acupuncture works – up to a point – (Daily Tele-graph *headline)*

The operation was a complete success, but the patient died of something else – *(John Chiene)*

Anyone who goes to see a psychiatrist should have his head examined – *(Anon)*

I can't stand whispering. Every time a doctor whispers in the hospital, next day there's a funeral – *(Anon)*

My doctor gave me six months to live, but when I couldn't pay he gave me six months more – *(Walter Matthau)*

Sometimes a tooth hurts so much it drives you to extraction – *(Anon)*

A cough so robust that I tapped into two new seams of phlegm – *(Bill Bryson)*

The next time you have a sore throat be glad you're not a giraffe – *(Anon)*

His halitosis was capable of de-scaling
a kettle at fifty paces
– *(Alan Coren)*

Medical discovery, it moves
in mighty leaps
It leapt straight past the common
cold and gave it us for keeps
– *(Pam Ayres)*

She got her looks from her father – he's a plastic surgeon – *(Groucho Marx)*

I have just heard about his illness; let's hope it is nothing trivial – *(Irvin Cobb)*

I am not yet by a great deal clear of my fit of the gout. It has made a long stay for so brief an acquaintance – *(Letter from Sydney Smith 1834)*

When I have gout I feel as if I am walking on my eyeballs – *(Sydney Smith)*

I gave up visiting my psychoanalyst because he was meddling too much in my private life – *(Tennessee Williams)*

The best medical speciality is dermatology. Your patients never call you out in the middle of the night, they never die of the disease, and they never get any better – *(Martin H. Fischer)*

The only parts of my original body are my elbows – *(Phyllis Diller)*

There must be something to acupuncture – after all, you never see any sick porcupines – *(Bob Goddard)*

I've just had an operation for piles – all my troubles are behind me – *(Ken Brett)*

He collected lists of fatal diseases and arranged them in alphabetical order so that he could put his finger without delay on any one he wanted to worry about – *(Joseph Heller)*

If this is what viral pneumonia does to one I really don't think I shall bother to have it again – *(Dame Gladys Cooper)*

Parishioner: My husband is in hospital having an operation on his piles.
Vicar: Poor man, he has had a rough passage this year!

People are sticking to Kleenex – *(Graffito)*

Patient: I keep thinking I'm a pair of curtains.
Doctor: For heaven's sake, woman, pull yourself together!

An elephant encountered a mouse. 'My,' said the elephant, 'you're a very small little thing, aren't you?' 'Yes,' agreed the mouse, 'but you see, I haven't been very well . . .'

Did you hear about the gynaecologist who papered the hall through the letterbox? – *(From a pub near Charing Cross Hospital, observed by Neil Kinnock 1982)*

After two days in hospital, I took a turn for the nurse – *(Rodney Dangerfield)*

I wouldn't be paranoid if people didn't pick on me – *(Anon)*

A neurosis is a secret you don't know you are keeping – *(Kenneth Tynan)*

A psychiatrist is a man who asks you a lot of expensive questions your wife asks you for nothing – *(Sam Bardell)*

A psychiatrist is a man who goes to a strip-show to watch the audience – *(Mervyn Stockwood)*

Psychoanalysis is the confessional of the agnostic – *(Anon)*

Hypochondria is the one disease I haven't got – *(Anon)*

MEMORY

Man remembers what God forgets – God remembers what man forgets – *(Anon)*

MONEY

Too many people spend money they don't have on things they don't want to impress people they don't like – *(Will Rogers quoted in Newsletter)*

My men, and I, suffer from a sickness of the heart that can only be cured by gold – *(Hernando Cortés – Spanish conquistador of Mexico)*

Money is better than poverty, if only for financial reasons – *(Woody Allen)*

Plenty of folks give the Lord credit – few give him cash! – *(Anon)*

Sanctified wealth is a rare commodity in America – *(D.L. Moody)*

Give God what's right, not what's left! – *(Anon)*

When God gives the order he always pays the bill – *(Anon)*

You should always live within your income, even if you have to borrow to do so – *(Josh Billings)*

If there's anyone to whom I owe money, I am prepared to forget it if they are – *(Errol Flynn)*

When one of the richest men in
the world – Howard Hughes, dies
of neglect . . . it spells the end
of the mystique of money
– (Malcolm Muggeridge)

How much did he leave? He left it all! – *(Anon)*

Bring your money here. You can't take it with you – *(Sign in grocer's shop)*

The man with the vision met the man with the money. The man with the money got the vision and the man with the vision got the money – *(Anon)*

Please do not ask Mr Shaw for money. He can write for you but he cannot finance you – *(George Bernard Shaw)*

I never met a rich man who was happy and I have only very occasionally met a poor man who did not want to become rich – *(Malcolm Muggeridge)*

The Church of England is a rule-bound place of strange practices, which just wants your money to promulgate a watered-down message – *(Representative group of non-church goers quizzed by Listening Groups 2000)*

Extravagance is the way the other fellow spends his money – *(Anon)*

Bills travel through the mail at twice the speed of cheques – *(Anon)*

The church is a good investment for your money – *(John Osteen)*

No one would remember the Good Samaritan if he had only had good intentions. He had money as well – *(Margaret Thatcher 6th January 1980)*

Money is a wonderful servant
but a terrible master
– *(Proverb)*

A bank is a place that will lend you money if you can prove that you don't need it – *(Bob Hope)*

I'm living so far beyond my income that we may almost be said to be living apart. – *(E.E. Cummings)*

In the midst of life we are in debt – (Ethel Mumford)

Three categories of people:
the haves,
the have-nots, and the
have-not-yet-paid-for-what-they-haves
– *(Anon)*

The way to a man's pocketbook is through his hobby – *(Anon)*

There are some things that money can't buy. For everything else there's a *Mastercard* – *(Anon)*

The government incomes policy is as significant as a blush on a dead man's cheek – *(Clive Jenkins)*

Money will buy you a beautiful dog, but only love will make it wag its tail – *(Anon)*

Money is like manure; it needs to be spread around widely if it is to do any lasting good – *(Anon)*

Takeovers are for the public good, but that's not why I do it. I do it to make money – *(Sir James Goldsmith* – Sunday Times *8th August 1985)*

Those who leave their money to God's work when they die instead of giving it now are more use to God dead than alive – *(Fred Mitchell)*

A budget is what you stay within if you don't want to go without – *(Anon)*

When you hear the word 'save' it is usually the beginning of an advertisement designed to make you spend money! – *(Anon)*

Money is frightening. It can serve or destroy man – *(Michel Quoist)*

The last thing to be converted is a man's pocket – *(Anon)*

One book that always has a sad ending is a cheque book – *(Anon)*

Nowadays we spend so much on luxuries we can't afford the necessities – *(Anon)*

We live expensively to impress people who live expensively to impress us – *(Anon)*

MONUMENT

The Dome must be the only symbolic monument to be erected without anyone having a clue what it is meant to symbolise – *(John McEwen* – Sunday Telegraph Review *2nd January 2000)*

MOTHER

You know more than you think you do – *(Benjamin Spock)*

William, you know so much – but I know so much better – *(Mother of future Archbishop William Temple)*

Nine out of ten working couples think children do better with mother at home – *(US Survey 2000)*

I love my mother in spite of her wrinkles – *(Stanley Jones)*

My mother told me I was born at night but I certainly was not born last night – *(Judge on TV in USA)*

GOOD WORK, MARY. WE ALL KNEW YOU HAD IT IN YOU –

(Dorothy Parker to Mrs Sherwood on the arrival of her baby)

Never run after a man or bus, darling – there'll always be another one five minutes later! – *(Anon)*

All women become like their mothers. That's their tragedy. No man does. That's his – *(Oscar Wilde)*

The party's over when motherhood begins – *(Headline in* Daily Telegraph *24th September 2000)*

St Augustine, 'the son of the tears of Monica' (his mother) – *(Anon)*

Ideally new mothers need their own mothers –
(Juliet Janvrin)

At Christmas time the kids hang up
their stockings and it will be a full
year before they ever hang up
anything else again!
– (Anon)

Educate children without faith and you create a race
of clever devils – *(Duke of Wellington)*

Having a baby is not an illness – *(Cindy Crawford)*

I have never got over the fact that I was born in bed
with a woman. – *(Wilson Mizner)*

Mother's love grows by giving
– (Charles Lamb)

A mother is only as happy as her child – *(Anon)*

Mother – that was the bank where we deposited all our hurts and worries – *(T. DeWitt Talmage)*

Of all the rights of women the greatest is to be a mother – *(Lin Yutang)*

Q. What is the greatest book you've ever read?
A. My mother! – *(Abraham Lincoln's reply)*

Women who seek to be equal with men lack ambition – *(Timothy Leary)*

A girl's best friend is her mother – *(Anon)*

If we accept that a mother can kill even her own child, how can we tell other people not to kill each other – *(Mother Teresa)*

Men are what their mothers made them – *(Ralph Waldo Emerson)*

The hand that rocks the cradle is the hand that rules the world – *(W.S. Ross)*

My mother was the source from which I derived the guiding principles of my life – *(John Wesley)*

God could not be everywhere so he made mothers – *(Yiddish Proverb)*

A mother who is really a mother is never free – *(Honoré de Balzac)*

The mother's heart is the child's schoolroom – *(Henry Ward Beecher)*

Who takes the child by the hand takes the mother by the heart – *(Danish Proverb)*

The precursor of the mirror is the mother's face –
(D.W. Winnicott)

A man may buy a house
but only a woman can make it a home
– *(Anon)*

The greatest love is a mother's, then comes a dog;
then comes a sweetheart – *(Polish Proverb)*

No work in the world pays like mother's work –
(Anon)

Unless you are prepared to pretend you don't have a
child: don't have a child – *(Advice of a working
mother – BBC Panorama 24th January 2000)*

A mother is not a person to lean on but
a person to make leaning unnecessary
– *(Dorothy Canfield Fisher)*

Mother nature is providential – she gives us twelve years to develop a love for our children before turning them into teenagers – *(Anon)*

How was it that you were born
in Scunthorpe?
Well you see, I thought it was
important to be near my mother
– *(Anon)*

Did you hear about the Irish girl who told her mother she was pregnant? The mother replied, 'Are you sure it's yours?' – *(Anon)*

Spiteful woman to mother of little girl: 'Oh what a pretty little girl! Is your husband good looking?' – *(Anon)*

MOTHER-IN-LAW

My mother-in-law's been coming round to our house at Christmas for the past seventeen years. This time we're thinking of letting her in – *(Anon)*

I took my mother-in-law to Madame Tussaud's Chamber of Horrors and one of the attendants said, 'Keep her moving – we're stocktaking' – *(Les Dawson)*

The maximum penalty for bigamy is two mothers-in-law – *(Anon)*

My mother-in-law had to stop skipping for exercise. It registered seven on the Richter Scale – *(Les Dawson)*

He had a very soft spot for his mother-in-law – a swamp – *(Anon)*

NANNY

Nanny required in the country for one boy, eighteen months old, non smoker – *(Advertisement in Cumberland News)*

NEIGHBOURS & NEIGHBOURHOOD

Nothing so ruins a neighbourhood as having an enthusiastic gardener next door – *(Anon)*

It is your own interest that is at stake when your next door neighbour's wall is ablaze – *(Horace)*

Good fences make good neighbours – *(Robert Frost)*

NOSTALGIA

If you are yearning for the good old days just switch off the air-conditioning – *(Griff Niblack)*

OLD AGE

Your secrets are safe with your friends because they can't remember them either – *(Anon)*

There's nothing left to learn the hard way – *(Anon)*

Things you buy now won't wear out – *(Anon)*

Never try to put your socks
on standing up
– (Advice of 89-year-old former Prime Minister Jim Callaghan to any man over seventy-five years of age)

Better to wear out than to rust out – *(Bishop Cumberland 1632–1718)*

I want to grow up before I grow old – *(John Wimber)*

OTHERS

No man is an island, entire of itself, every man is a piece of the continent, a part of the main – *(John Donne)*

Don't try to impress others: let them impress you! – *(Anon)*

Don't ever assume people know how you feel about them. Tell them! Nobody can be told too often that he or she is loved – *(Anon)*

We should ask ourselves what the man on the Clapham omnibus would think – *(Lord Brown)*

Instead of putting others in their place, try putting yourself in their place occasionally – *(Anon)*

Your gift blesses others – your giving blesses you – *(Anon)*

The more I get to know people, the more I love my dog – *(Frederick the Great)*

It is well to remember that the entire population of the universe, with one trifling exception, is composed of others – *(J.A. Holmes)*

Taint is a mutual matter. We are touched by each other's . . . failures – *(Bishop Peter Selby)*

The greatest achievements are those that benefit others – *(Anon)*

It took me a long time not to judge myself through the eyes of someone else – *(Anon)*

The best conversationalist is the person who lets others do the talking – *(Anon)*

PARENTING

Parents are the very last people who ought to be allowed to have children – *(Ted Bell)*

Q. What do you want your next child to be?
A. A grandchild – *(Anon)*

Parenting needs perseverance
– *(Juliet Janvrin)*

Parents aren't interested in justice, they're interested in quiet – *(Bill Crosby)*

There are times when parenthood seems nothing but feeding the hand that bites you – *(Peter de Vries)*

Parents learn a lot from their children about coping with life – *(Muriel Spark)*

Whilst you are getting ready to take me out Dad, I'll be waiting outside getting older! – *(Small boy)*

The best heritage a father can leave is a good example – *(Anon)*

Our children are like mirrors – they reflect our attitudes in life – *(Anon)*

It is a wise father that knows his own child – *(William Shakespeare in* The Merchant of Venice)

. . . fathers, provoke not your children – *(St Paul – Ephesians 6:4 – KJV)*

To lose one parent, Mr Worthing, may be regarded as a misfortune; to lose both looks like carelessness – *(Oscar Wilde in* The Importance of Being Earnest*)*

PESTS

Among the things we don't understand is how a mosquito can get along without any sleep – *(Anon)*

PETS

A door is what a dog is perpetually on the wrong side of – *(Ogden Nash)*

Dogs are sons of bitches – *(W.C. Fields)*

Cats seem to go on the principle that it never does any harm to ask for what you want – *(Joseph Woods Krutch)*

Dog wins top prize at Crufts – *(Buckingham Advertiser)*

The indefatigable and unsavoury engine of pollution – the dog – *(John Sparrow)*

Please do not feed animals. If you
have any suitable food, give it
to the guard on duty
– *(Sign in Budapest Zoo)*

POSSESSIONS

If it takes you more than fifteen minutes to pack, you have too much stuff – *(Mother Teresa)*

Whatever we possess becomes of double value when we share it with others – *(Anon)*

If we can't have the best of everything we can make the best of everything we have – *(Anon)*

Precociousness

Thank you, Madam, the agony is very much abated – *(Lord Macaulay, aged 4, having had hot coffee spilt over his legs)*

Quarrel

These two ladies will never agree: they are arguing from different premises – *(Sydney Smith)*

Quarrels would not last long if the fault were only on one side – *(La Rochefoucauld)*

Rest

Go to sleep in peace. God is awake – *(Victor Hugo)*

It was Einstein who made the real trouble. He announced in 1905 that there was no such thing as absolute rest. After that there never was – *(Stephen Leacock)*

How blessed it is to do nothing and to rest after it – *(Persian Proverb)*

Have a little relaxation for when you come back to your work your judgement will be surer – *(Leonardo da Vinci)*

RETIREMENT

Asked about when he might retire the ageing Lord Chief Justice Denning replied that he had been told that he had every virtue except that of resignation – *(TV interview)*

When a man retires and time is no
longer a matter of importance
– his colleagues generally present
him with a watch
– *(R.C. Sheriff)*

I would like to retire before becoming famous – *(George Harrison – ex-Beatles)*

Ex-Prime Ministers are like untethered ships in the harbour – they just bang about doing a lot of damage – *(W.E. Gladstone)*

I want to get out with my greatness intact – *(Muhammad Ali in* The Observer *1974)*

ROMANCE

Love is like the measles – all the worse when it comes late in life – *(Douglas Jarrold)*

So I fell in love with a rich attorney's
Elderly ugly daughter
– *(W.S. Gilbert)*

Tell me George, if you had to do it all over would you fall in love with yourself again? – *(Oscar Wilde)*

The magic of first love is our ignorance that it can ever end – *(Benjamin Disraeli)*

SCHOOL, SCHOOLCHILDREN

Please excuse Johnny from being absent as I was having a baby – and it's not his fault! – *(Parent's note to a teacher)*

A virgin forest is a forest in which the hand of man has never set foot – *(Schoolboy howler)*

Will the boy who borrowed the steps from the school caretaker last month please return them otherwise further steps will be taken – *(School notice board)*

The cold at the North Pole is so great that the towns there are not inhabited – *(Schoolboy howler)*

Pompeii was destroyed by an overflow of saliva from the Vatican – *(K.F. Banner)*

After his divorce from Catherine of Aragon, Henry VIII married Anne Boleyn, and Archbishop Cranmer consummated the marriage – *(Schoolboy howler)*

To prevent milk from going sour keep it in the cow – *(Schoolboy howler)*

The blood circulates to the lower limbs by going down one leg and up the other – *(Schoolboy howler)*

Trees break wind for up to 200 metres – *(Schoolboy howler)*

Vacuum: a large empty space where the Pope lives – *(Schoolboy howler)*

A fossil is an extinct animal. The older it is, the more extinct it is – *(Schoolboy howler)*

Water is composed of two gins. Oxygin is pure gin. Hydrogin is gin and water – *(Schoolboy howler)*

The Fallopian tube is named after the monk who first discovered it – *(Schoolboy howler)*

The little boy at the zoo stared at the stork for a long time, then turned to his father and said, 'Gosh, Dad, he doesn't recognise me.' – *(Anon)*

SEX

Fire needs a fireplace: sex needs marriage – *(Andy Comiskey)*

. . . the excessive preoccupation with erotica in a society dedicated to carnality spells the end of the mystique of sex
— *(Malcolm Muggeridge)*

Lord give me chastity, but not yet – *(The young St Augustine of Hippo)*

For millions of people the erotic has completely displaced the spiritual – *(A.W. Tozer)*

I blame my father for telling me about the birds and the bees. I was going steady with a woodpecker for two years
– *(Bob Hope)*

They made love as though they were an endangered species – *(Peter de Vries)*

We used the rhythm method but kept missing the beat – *(Father of ten children)*

Contraceptives should be used on every conceivable occasion
– *(Spike Milligan)*

Sex is an act which on sober reflection one recalls with repugnance and in a more elevated mood even with disgust – *(A. Schopenhauer)*

The English have sex on the brain – which is a frightfully uncomfortable place to have it – *(Malcolm Muggeridge)*

There is a certain fury in sex that we cannot afford to inflame, and a certain mystery and awe must surround it if we are to remain sane – *(G.K. Chesterton)*

Everybody knows that I do not like excessive sex – *(Ann Widdecombe* – Daily Telegraph *2nd April 2000)*

I am the Love that dare not speak its name – *(Lord Alfred Douglas involved in the Oscar Wilde scandal)*

SINGLE LIFE STYLE

(He was) . . . practising celibacy openly in the streets – *(Criticism of minister for walking across from his rectory to the church in a cassock)*

Civilisation depends for its existence and development upon some restraint of the most urgent sexual drives – *(Sigmund Freud)*

The hardest aspect is not doing without sex, but the lack of intimacy – *(Fr Timothy Radcliffe – Master of the Dominican Order)*

SLEEP & WAKING

Remember that by fifty you will have spent over sixteen years in bed and three years eating – *(Anon)*

I have so much to do that I'm going to bed – *(Robert Benchley)*

If you can't sleep, don't count sheep . . . talk to the Shepherd – *(Anon)*

Laugh and the world laughs with you. Snore and you sleep alone – *(Anthony Burgess)*

Sleep with clean hands, either kept clean all day by integrity or washed clean at night by repentance – *(John Donne)*

The best cure for insomnia is to get a lot of sleep
– *(W.C. Fields)*

How did you find yourself this morning? – *(Irish hostess)*

Did ye heer the news this morning? The Holy Father woke up dead! – *(Irish landlady to guest)*

The only good that comes from the east is the sun – *(Traditional Portuguese Saying)*

I just rolled back the sheets and there I was – *(Anon)*

Sleep is when all the unsorted stuff comes flying out as from a dustbin upset in a high wind – *(William Golding)*

The lion and the lamb shall lie down together, but the lamb won't get much sleep – *(Anon)*

TEENAGERS

Nowadays the voice crying in the wilderness is just a teenager with a mobile phone – *(Anon)*

Teenagers learn to manage money by being given money to manage – *(Anon)*

Teenagers are risk-takers, but they can't always assess the risk – *(Juliet Janvrin)*

A teenager is grown up when he thinks it is more important to pass an examination than to pass the car ahead – *(Anon)*

Raising teenagers is like nailing Jelly to a tree –
(Anon)

My son had taken up meditation – at least it's better
than sitting around doing nothing – *(Max
Kauffman)*

Q. If you had no feet would you be
wearing shoes?
A. Of course not – how ridiculous!
Q. Then why are you wearing a bra?
– *(Scornful 14-year-old girl to 12-year-old sister)*

When the world is awake the teenager slumbers –
(Juliet Janvrin)

Meal time is when the youngsters continue eating
but sit down – *(Anon)*

Telling a teenage the facts of life is like giving a fish
a bath – *(Anon)*

When I was sixteen my father was an ignoramus; but when I was twenty-one I was surprised at how much progress the old man had made – *(Mark Twain)*

It's all the young can do for the old, to shock them and keep them up to date – *(Anon)*

Until I was thirteen I thought my name was 'shut up' – *(Joe Namath)*

My father would never take me to the zoo. He said if they wanted me they would come and get me – *(Rodney Dangerfield)*

Any astronomer can predict with absolute accuracy just where every star in the universe will be at 11.30 tonight. He can make no such prediction about his teenage daughter – *(James T. Adams)*

Seventy-five per cent of teens allowed peer pressure to override their own better judgement – *(Psychologist Dr Ruth Berenda's research group)*

It's easy for you, Dad; you've had all your problems! – *(Teenage daughter)*

Son: Mum, you know that vase you were worried I might break?
Mother: Yes, what about it?
Son: Well, your worries are over!

My son Martin's gone all lefty, and of the crappiest naturalist kind. He's bright you see but a fool – *(Kingsley Amis writing to Philip Larkin)*

Watching your daughter being collected by her date feels like handing over a million dollar Stradivarius to a gorilla – *(Jim Bishop)*

Adolescence is the stage between puberty and adultery – *(Crosbie's Dictionary of Puns)*

Never criticise other people's teenagers. You never know how yours will turn out – *(Juliet Janvrin)*

Teenagers need to be self-centred in order to discover their sense of self – *(Juliet Janvrin)*

Teenagers and moderation rarely mix – *(Juliet Janvrin)*

My salad days, when I was green in judgement – *(Shakespeare in* Antony and Cleopatra*)*

Teenager's highest priority is their social life – *(Juliet Janvrin)*

My son is going through one of those awkward stages . . . from hooligan to layabout – *(Resigned mother)*

A teenage daughter seems to have to find many aspects of her father ridiculous before she can make sense of another man – *(Juliet Janvrin)*

Cain was a juvenile delinquent without being born on the wrong side of the tracks – *(Anon)*

If you are not dogmatic at twenty you will have no convictions at forty – *(Basil Gough)*

God will always use young people to do his work because they will get the job done before they know it can't be done – *(Loren Cunningham – founder of Youth With A Mission)*

Your ministry can be summed up in five words. Love God and love youth. Period – *(Ricardo Crisco – Youth Pastor – Brownsville, Pensacola)*

The great majority of youth offenders are males, without fathers involved in their lives. Many have never even met their fathers – *(Newsweek)*

Winning an argument should never mean more to a parent than winning the child – *(Juliet Janvrin)*

TELEPHONE

Have you ever noticed that wrong numbers are never engaged? – *(Steven Wright)*

Well, if I called the wrong number, why did you answer the phone? – *(Anon)*

Wrong idiot, you number! – *(Anon response to mis-dialled phone call)*

The hills are alive with the sound of mobiles – (Daily Telegraph *headline – 2nd November 2000)*

TIDINESS

A filing cabinet is a place where you can lose things systematically – *(T.H. Thompson)*

He's fanatically tidy . . . Do you know, after he takes a bath he washes the soap – *(Hugh Leonard)*

VEGETARIAN

A vegetarian is not nice – to meat
– *(Anon)*

WASTE

Waste not – want not – *(Proverb)*

The longer one saves something before throwing it away, the sooner it will be needed after it is thrown away – *(Anon)*

Extravagance is the way the other fellow spends his money – *(Anon)*

WEATHER

When two Englishmen meet, their first talk is of the weather – *(Samuel Johnson)*

All of us could learn a lot from the weather – it pays no attention to criticism – *(Anon)*

He is not leaving under a cloud – *(A Met office spokesman on the resignation of John Kettley, the BBC weatherman)*

Thank heavens the sun has gone in and I don't have to go out and enjoy it – *(Logan Pearsall Smith)*

Everybody talks about the weather, but nobody does anything about it – *(Charles D. Warner)*

Widespread fist and mog can be expected
– *(Weather bloomer)*

Overnight parts of England received
111mm of rainfall, while Nice in France
received 5 inches – *(BBC forecaster)*

The English winter – ending in July. To
recommence in August – *(Byron* – Don
Juan*)*

Summer has set in with its usual severity
– *(Samuel Taylor Coleridge)*

Some are weatherwise, some are
otherwise – *(Benjamin Franklin)*

It was such a lovely day I thought it was
a pity to get up – *(Somerset Maugham)*

WOMAN

I know I have the body of a weak and feeble woman but I have the heart and stomach of a king and of a king of England too – *(Queen Elizabeth I)*

They call her 'Appendix' . . . if you take her out once, that's enough – *(Anon)*

Darling, you look absolutely beautiful this morning – it must have taken you ages – *(Anon)*

I always say that if you want a speech made you should ask a man but if you want something done you should ask a woman – *(Margaret Thatcher)*

She was another of those near Mrs – *(Alfred McFote)*

If you want to win her hand,
Let the maiden understand
That she's not the only
pebble on the beach
– *(Harry Braisted)*

Better to be looked over than to be overlooked –
(Mae West)

Woman's ambition – to be weighed and found
wanting – *(Anon)*

She's an angel . . . always up in the air and harping
on something – *(Anon)*

My economic philosophy is middle of the road. I
spend money left, right and centre – *(Woman to
neighbour)*

SOS – LSD – RSVP – *(Telegram sent to
her father when she was short of cash, from
Elizabeth Bowes Lyon, later Queen and
then Queen Mother, when still a young
lady)*

Somewhere on this earth, a woman gives birth to a
child every ten seconds. We must find this woman
and stop her at once – *(Sam Levenson)*

Behind every great man stands an astonished woman – *(Anon)*

He was well gutted, but I was more gutted-er than he was – *(Anon)*

She was never really charming until she died – *(Terence)*

Well today was a total waste of make-up – *(Businesswomen)*

She is as tough as an ox. She will be turned into Bovril when she dies – *(Anon)*

Hell hath no fury like a woman scorned – *(William Shakespeare)*

She was so dramatic she stabbed the potatoes at dinner – *(Sydney Smith)*

Her vocabulary is small, but the turnover is terrific – *(Anon)*

Women have very little idea of how much men hate them – *(Germaine Greer in* The Female Eunuch *1971)*

Generally speaking, she's generally speaking – *(Anon)*

She's so tired at the end of the day she can hardly keep her mouth open – *(Anon)*

She has a keen sense of rumour – *(Anon)*

She ran the gamut of emotions from A to B
– (Dorothy Parker of Katherine Hepburn's acting in a play in 1934)

We have taken this action because as women . . . it is our duty, even to break the law, in order to call attention to the reasons why we do so – *(Emmeline Pankhurst – suffragette in court 21st October 1908)*

She who must be obeyed – *(Rider Haggard – in the novel* She *– 1887)*

We are not ashamed of what we have done, because, when you have a great cause to fight for, the moment of greatest humiliation is the moment when the spirit is proudest – *(Christabel Pankhurst – suffragette – speech 19th March 1908)*

Never in the history of fashion has so little material been raised so high to reveal so much that needs to be covered so badly – *(Cecil Beaton)*

Fashion anticipates, and elegance is a state of mind – *(Oleg Cassini)*

A lot of things considered de rigueur thirty years ago are considered deplorable today – *(Anon)*

A fur collar is capable of things dungarees can only dream of – *(Philip Delves Broughton)*

Fat is a feminist issue – *(Susie Orbach –
1978)*

She could eat an apple through a tennis
racquet – *(Noel Coward –* Come into the
Garden Maud*)*

Two of the nicest people if ever there was
one – *(Alan Bennett on Sidney and
Beatrice Webb)*

Contrary to popular belief English
women do not wear tweed nightgowns –
(Hermione Gingold)

There is a tide in the affairs of women
which taken at the flood, leads –
goodness knows where! – *(Anon)*

When women kiss, it always reminds me of prize-fighters shaking hands – *(H.L. Mencken)*

For the female of the species is more deadly than the male – *(Rudyard Kipling* – The Female of the Species*)*

I heard a man say that brigands demand your money or your life, whereas women require both – *(Samuel Butler)*

Would you rather be in the light with the wise virgins or in the dark with the foolish ones? – *(Anon)*

That woman speaks eighteen languages
and can't say 'no' in any of them
– *(Dorothy Parker)*

A woman seldom writes her mind but in a postscript
– *(Richard Steele)*

She was a continuous puzzle without any solution –
(Billy Wilder of Marilyn Monroe)

My mother-in-law had to stop skipping for exercise. It registered seven on the Richter Scale – *(Les Dawson)*

I didn't hire Scott as assistant coach because he's my son. I hired him because I married his mother – *(Frank Layden)*

What a blonde – she was enough to make a bishop kick a hole in a stained glass window – *(Raymond Chandler)*

My wife's idea of double parking is to park her car on top of another car – *(Shelley Berman)*

She could very well pass for forty-three, in the dusk with a light behind her – *(W.S. Gilbert)*

Outside every thin woman is a fat woman trying to get in – *(Katharine Whitehorn)*

She had curves in places where other people don't even have places – *(Cybill Shepherd of Marilyn Monroe)*

Men of every age flocked around Diana Cooper like gulls round a council tip – *(John Carey)*

A woman without a man is like a fish without a bicycle – *(Graffito at Birmingham University)*

A woman needs a man like a fish needs a bicycle – *(Attributed to legendary feminist Ms Gloria Steinem who has recently married)*

A woman is like a tea bag. You can't tell how strong she is until you put her in hot water

– *(Nancy Reagan)*

One of my friends who is happily married has a husband so ugly she met him when a friend sent him over to her house to cure her hiccoughs – *(Phyllis Diller)*

A woman won a prize for identifying her most useful gadget – she said it was her husband – *(Anon)*

You don't know a woman until you have met her – in court – *(Norman Mailer)*

Hearing nuns' confessions is like being stoned to death with popcorn – *(Father J. Sheen)*

Her smile is so radiant that I believe it would force even a gooseberry bush into flower – *(Sydney Smith)*

The lady doth protest too much methinks – *(William Shakespeare)*

My wife is not suspicious – she knows – *(Anon)*

I haven't reported my missing credit card to the police because whoever stole it is spending less than my wife – *(Illie Nastase)*

The most effective way to remember your wife's birthday is to forget it once – *(Anon)*

Sir! A woman preaching is like a dog walking on its hind legs. You don't expect it to be done well – you are surprised to find it done at all
– *(Samuel Johnson)*

WORRY

Worry is the darkroom in which 'negatives' are developed – *(Anon)*

All worry is calculating without God
– *(Oswald Chambers)*

A minute of extra thinking beforehand can save hours of extra worry later – *(Anon)*

Worry is like a rocking chair. It gives you something to do but it gets you nowhere – *(Anon)*

I have a new philosophy – I'm only going to dread one day at a time – *(Anon)*

If you are going to pray don't worry. If you are going to worry, don't pray – *(Old Jamaican Proverb)*

Of all your worries great or small, the worst of them never happened at all – *(Anon)*

YOUTH

It is against the natural order of things for those who are youngest, with the least experience of life, to have the greatest influence in directing the life of society – *(Alexander Solzhenitsyn – BBC Panorama interview March 1976)*

Being young is not having any money; being young is not minding not having any money – *(Katherine Whitehouse)*